Grand Legacy

of Regal Years

This book belongs

Grand Legacy

of Regal Years

Helping Grandchildren Know Their Grandparents Better

By Martin Stevens

Acknowledgements

I would like to acknowledge my Creator God, the supreme spark of our lives. He truly deserves all the *G.L.o.R.Y*. To my wife and children, my godchildren, nieces and nephews, extended family and friends ... who are few, but you know who you are.

A big salute to my late grandparents and the loving, lasting legacy they leave behind, even though my knowledge and memories of them are very limited, the effect of their existence lives on through the lives of the grandchildren from their 10 children.

In Loving Memory of my grandma and granddad

Disclaimer

This 'Open Diary' is not necessarily exclusive to grandparents alone, as it may well be of benefit and a blessing to parents or great grandparents as well.

In fact, it doesn't even have to be restricted to blood family members, as it may well be a great source of help and / or encouragement to anyone who desires to bless someone else with their legacy. In other words, if a business owner desires to leave a new business idea to their friend's child, niece, nephew or godchild, they may very well see this as a great resource to do so. Not in a legal way, as there are other procedures for such a thing, but just as an easy to be transparent.

*The concept of this 'Open Diary' is built around the cultural tradition of individuals leaving an inheritance for the children of their own children. See **Proverbs 13:22**) and as we live in a world where we never know how long we have left, I desire for us to capture and cherish what we can from that generation, whilst we are able to do so.*

Meet the Author

This book is Martin's second publication, following hot on the heals of his personal development and community rebuilding project 'Raising Up Role Models'.

Martin Stevens assures us that, as long as life allows, there will be several more power-packed and content rich books to follow over the next 5 - 10 years.

Here he presents to you Grand Legacy of Regal Years, which is the result of, a concept inspired by Prov. 13:22, a conversation and the passing of Two Queens.

Author: Martin Stevens

I am **Martin Stevens**, I am a husband, a father of three sons, a godfather to 7 godchildren and a few unofficial ones, a mentor, and a rather creative individual that is always noting down ideas and lyrics. I am also the Founding Director of a Social Enterprise P.A.D **(Progression And Development)**.

My passion and mission include helping to strengthen and rebuild the family bonds between godparents and all of their godchildren, and now more recently, helping to highlight and bridge the important gap between grandparent(s) and (pending) grandchild(ren).

For the foreword of this project, I needed to enlist the best suited individual to review this 'Open-Diary' styled book. Someone who not only understood the mission and could see the vision but could also understand from a perspective of seeing the real impact of witnessing the benefits of how important a grandparent's life is to their grandchild(ren). This list was still not whittled down to one person at this point, as there are so many people who can testify to this.

However, when I reflected on the funeral of one Mother Magdalene Thompson and how so many brethren from across the UK came down in her honour to say their farewell, even referring to her as Queen Magdalene, plus I was honoured to have been drafted as a Guard of Honour on duty for her regal casket, I knew then that it was the daughter of the late Pastor and Mother Thompson, the elegant, the orator, the ambassador of children's Summer School education, also a mother, godmother and auntie to those who also looked up to their grandmother with fond memories, none other than Lady Fiona Fuller, who paid a most beautiful and royal tribute to her mother and friend, 'Queen' Mother Magdalene Thompson.

Foreword: Fiona Fuller

"Grandparents are voices of the past and the door to the future. They provide us with the wisdom from a lifetime of experience that should never be undervalued" *author unknown*.

The family is the foundation on which society is based and Grandparents are a wonderful asset to any. Their stories can help youngsters, who may be struggling with their own identity, discover who they truly are, give them the knowledge of belonging and help them gain inspiration to become great, **indeed a grandparent's story can raise a generation of world changers.**

The wealth of knowledge grandparents hold is immeasurable, their appreciation of life which for many is borne out of hardship, provide them with a unique wisdom and insight on the plethora of challenges life often throws at us.

It's fair to say Grandparents love nothing more than sharing their life stories, immersing themselves and the listener into their memories and experiences, and "Grand Legacy of Regal Years" provides a beautiful way for families to preserve their own unique and *unsubstitutable* record of these stories. If you're unsure where to start, then the open-diary format of this book with its handy headings gives focal points and ideas for conversations.

There are also practical sections; 'The importance of Prayer' highlights this beautiful gift God has given us and one which many Grandparents relied on to get them through tough times, answers to questions of who we are and where we come from, and meaning to the marvellous traditions they hold dear and the sporadic 'one-liners' Grandparents throw in from time to time, can be responded to in the section entitled 'My Life's Journey'.

A cohesive family encourages strong social values, respect and appreciation for others, and Martin Stevens, who possesses an exuberant drive and commitment to persevering family values, has given us a practical tool to help us protect those family values and ideals, in a format that's easy to keep and pass on, for generations to treasure for years to come.

Thank you, Mr Stevens.

Table of Contents

Acknowledgements 5

Disclaimer 7

Meet the Author 8

    Author: Martin Stevens... 8

    Foreword: Fiona Fuller 9

Table of Contents... 10

An Inheritance for your children's children 14

About Grand Legacy.. 16

Definitions 17

    Who I Am 22

Conversations with Parents, Grandparents & Grandkids..... 26

Life's Journey - Childhood 32

Favourite Things 46

Adopt A Grandparent 54

Cost vs Value.. 57

Things I Can Teach You 60

    How to Pray Effectively 62

Family Tree Lineage 68

2022 / 2023 Calendar 78

Space for Photos 80

My Life's Journey – Continued... 84

Eulogies.. 98

    What is a Eulogy? 98

Eulogy Template(s) 99

When I Transition 100

    Poem: Separated 124

How to Handle Grief, Guilt and Bereavement 125

A Directory 128

   List of Financial Service Providers 129

   List of Debt Solution Services 131

   List of Fun Activities 131

   List of Grandparent Services 133

   List of Pet Services 133

   List of Ancestry Services 133

   List of Youth Development Organisations 134

   List of Maths and English Tutors 134

   List of Fashion, Accessories and Gifts 136

   List of Nail Technicians 136

   List of Hair and Beauty Provision 137

   List of Herbs and Health Care 139

   List of Confidential Counsellors 139

   List of Child and Family Support Organisations 140

   Larger List via Online Directories 140

   List of Local Community Projects in Croydon 144

   List of Community Organisations 145

   List of Online Christian Dating Services + ... 146

   List of Life Saving Services 146

   List of Funeral Services 147

   In loving memory of loved ones gone on before. 147

Celebrating their G.L.o.R.Y 148

Thank you all 149

   Other people, organisations or services you know and recommend ... 150

References 152

During the journey of writing 'Raising Up Role Models', a personal development workbook for those whose have the honourable title of 'Godparent', I often came across comments or had people mishear me and assume that I was meant to be referring to 'Grandparents'. It was along this path, that some smoulders of an idea started to form about providing something for grandparents but couldn't quite grasp what that would or should be.

It was only whilst I was in a conversation with a lady who said that she is writing a book, but only for her grandchildren, that the concept finally landed for me. A book that grandparents can utilise like an 'open diary' for the benefit of their grandchildren to read, that would kind of serve as a source of information, insight to the family heritage and possibly even as an aide for a eulogy.

This book would serve as an opportunity for parents, grandparents and possibly even great grandparents to record memories of events, special dates and memorable moments in time, that their grandchildren might be too young at the time to appreciate. This would then therefore become a great heirloom or a contender for a time-capsule experience. Time-capsule experiments are the results of placing several items that represent the current age, placing them into a box, container or suitcase, then locking it away or burying it, with the intention of it not being opened for a decade.

Imagine that a time-capsule suitcase had been locked away by your grandparents for you, and when you opened it, inside you found a tape cassette, VHS cassette, vinyl records, a telegram and a pager. How many of those items are you aware of? If none, then take the time to check them out on Google images. This is a privilege that your grandparents never would have had back in the 60's, 70's and 80's, probably not even in the 90's either. Well, with the way that technology evolves so quickly, who knows what things will have disappeared and become the new norm in the next decade or so.

**And so, here I present to you 'Grand Legacy: of Regal Years',
as a love gift from Grandparent(s) to Grandchild(ren).**

Thank you for choosing and purchasing this book

These numbers are for your colouring pleasure.

An Inheritance for your children's children

As you may have gathered from the chapter title, it refers to grandparents. However, before I go further, let me offer a definition of the word 'Inheritance'.

The word 'Inheritance' derives from the word 'Inherit', which I understand to indicate that a person (usually a sibling or an offspring) receives something from another family member, almost by default of some kind of incident or occurrence. This can be almost anything ranging from a biological condition or an orphaned child to a house, business or windfall of money. Let's see what the dictionary says.

The definition of 'Inheritance' according to the Merriam-Webster Dictionary is:

1: **something that is or may be inherited**.
2: a: the act of inheriting property. b: the reception of genetic qualities by transmission from parent to offspring. c: the acquisition of a possession, condition, or trait from past generations.
(Definition of inheritance, n.d.)

The phrase 'An Inheritance to your children's children' comes from the Bible.

A good *man* leaves an inheritance to his children's children,
But the wealth of the sinner is stored up for the righteous.

Proverbs 13:22 NKJV

The *EasyEnglish* Bible records the scripture as …

When a good man dies, his grandchildren get his money.
But a sinner's money will go to those who are good.

EasyEnglish (Proverb 13:22, n.d.)

Let me also state that, although the scripture says 'man' and 'his', today it can be interchanged with 'woman' and 'her' or more simply, 'person' and 'their'.

Ok, now with that cleared up and out of the way, let's dive a little deeper into the custom of their day and what this phrase is pointing out to us today.

A good translation of what this scripture / statement is getting at is, parents ought to have the mindset of planning for the children of their own children. If I condition myself to think and plan far enough ahead to account for the wealth and wellbeing of my grandchildren, especially if I can do this way before they are even born, it would be very wise indeed.

However, I don't what you to think or feel that this should be viewed as a way to overlook the wealth accumulation or wellbeing of your own children or your great grandchildren, but rather see it a way of possibly letting your children know that they still ought to work, upskill and pursue their own personal goals and ambitions, striving to do the same for their own future generations as well.

At this point, I would quickly like to draw attention to the fact that 'wealth' does not mean 'money', it simply means to have plenty or a good amount of something. Examples can include Knowledge, Understanding, Connections, Experience, Love, Books, Music, Skills, Wisdom, etc.   … oh and Money.

Job 12:12 ≣

BBE Old men have wisdom, and a long life gives knowledge.

EasyEnglish Old people are often *wise. And they understand more things if they live for a long time.

ISV "Wisdom may be found in the company of the aged. Understanding comes with longevity.

The book of Job lets us know in the 12th chapter and 12th verse that "With the ancient is wisdom and inn length of days understanding". See translations of that KJV (King James Version) above. However, that scripture should not be misinterpreted as though it is true of everyone. King David wrote in Psalms 90:10 that "The aged aren't always wise, nor do the elderly always understand justice". And this is where the roles can sometimes be reversed, especially in this internet and technologically advanced age of society, there is plenty that our senior folks can learn from the younger generation born into this high-speed, futuristic era.

About Grand Legacy

I didn't give too much attention to wanting to write a book solely for grandparents, as I felt that the strategies within 'Raising Up Role Models' would be sufficient to adapt. This was until a had a conversation with a lady who told me that she was going to publish a book that she is writing … however, she only planned to make 2 copies, just for her grandchildren, then she would remove it. I pressed her on this point and she was adamant that it was going to be just for her grandchildren. This made sense, as she would personalise the book with information that would not be for the world to read, I get it … but that's when the lightbulb clicked on for me.

This book, Grand Legacy, aims to encourage powerful, informative and inspirational conversations, bridging the gap between grandparents and their grandchildren.

The name for the book came simply from the focus of passing on legacies from grandparents to grandchildren, as mentioned in Prov. 13:22. The legacy of our grandparents ought to be noted, if not documented, but how should they do this? This is where my book comes in. Grand Legacy will act as an 'Open Diary', meaning, it is there to be used and filled in with personal testimonials and stories, etc, that can be passed on to their children's children.

Then there is the full name of the book. Well, I am a lover of acronyms, so once I saw that the first two letters were 'G' & 'L', I gave some thought as to what acronym I could possibly create from this. Something that would complement the concept and represent something dynamic for the grandparents. This challenge to write and complete a new book within 2 months only started one week into the month of September. During the time that The Queen Mother died, we only saw nothing but 24 hours of news about the royal family and Queen Elizabeth's life history. That's when I was inspired with the Royal / Regal part of the name.

Our grand folks are indeed special, royal and precious to us, but royals (as in the monarchy) are different from most, so choosing 'Regal' was easy, and thus '**G**rand **L**egacy **o**f **R**egal **Y**ears' was born.   Have you noticed the acronym yet? 😊

Definitions

Grand

grand *adjective* (SPLENDID)

impressive and large or important:

- *The Palace of Versailles is very grand.*
- *They always entertain their guests in grand style.*

Used in the name of a place or building to show that it is large or beautiful and deserves to be admired:

the Grand Hotel, the Grand Canyon, the Grand Canal

grand *adjective* (EXCELLENT)

old-fashioned informal or Irish English

excellent or enjoyable:

- *We had grand weather on our holiday.*
- *My grandson is a grand little chap.*
- *You've done a grand job.*

grand *noun* [C] (MONEY)

informal

£1,000:

- *John's new car cost him 20 grand!*

(Grand, n.d.)

Legacy

noun [C]

money or property that you receive from someone after they die:

- *An elderly cousin had **left** her a small legacy.*

something that is a part of your history or that remains from an earlier time:

The Greeks have a rich legacy of literature.

The war has left a legacy of hatred.

More examples

- *The scars are the legacy of chicken pox.*
- *I received a small legacy from an aunt.*
- *The novel will be his legacy*

A legacy is also money or property left to a person by someone who has died.

(Legacy, n.d.)

Regal

adjective

very <u>special</u> and <u>suitable</u> for a <u>king</u> or <u>queen</u>:

- a regal <u>manner</u>
- He made a regal <u>entrance</u>.

Synonym

<u>majestic</u>

Compare

<u>imperial</u>

<u>royal</u> *adjective*

<u>kingly</u>

<u>queenly</u>

(Regal, n.d.)

Years

a <u>long</u> <u>time</u>:

It's taken years to get <u>funding</u> for the <u>project</u>.

He's been doing the same <u>job</u> **for years**.

(Years, n.d.)

Who I Am

My name:	Date of Birth: / /
Your other grandparent's name:	
My place of birth:	
Hospital:	
The place I grew up in:	

My Primary School
My Secondary School
My College:
My University:

My favourite Subject(s):
My Local Parks:

My Friends / Key Associates were:

Any other info

_____
_____
_____
_____
_____
_____
_____
_____
_____
_____
_____
_____
_____
_____
_____
_____
_____
_____
_____
_____
_____

Conversations with Parents, Grandparents & Grandkids

Testimonials

_____

_____

_____

_____

_____

_____

_____

_____

_____

_____

_____

_____

_____

_____

_____

_____

_____

_____

_____

_____

Life's Journey - Childhood
Upbringing, Schooling, WW2, teenage years, dating, employment, **Windrush**, etc.

Favourite Things

Here is a list of some of my favourite things that I enjoy now and did back then.

Books

_____

_____

_____

_____

_____

_____

_____

_____

_____

_____

_____

_____

_____

_____

_____

_____

_____

_____

Food

_____

_____

_____

_____

_____

_____

_____

_____

_____

_____

_____

_____

_____

_____

_____

_____

_____

_____

_____

_____

Films

_____

_____

_____

_____

_____

_____

_____

_____

_____

_____

_____

_____

_____

_____

_____

_____

_____

_____

_____

_____

Music Artists / Albums

Bible Scriptures

Other favourites, like TV shows, restaurants, museums, sports, hobbies, etc.

Adopt A Grandparent

Name:	**Adopt A Grandparent**	*(London)*
Service:	*Combating loneliness by connecting youngsters with senior citizens.*	
Contact:	*E: AdoptAGrandparent@Picpr.com*	
Details:	*W: www.AdoptAGrandparent.org.uk*	*T: 01386 882 474*

Whilst this workbook aims to better connect all grandparents with their grandchildren, there is also actually a large community of grandparents that are alone, able and willing to be paired up with a young person who also desires to connect with someone who can allow them to experience an exchange of time and expressions of care from someone who will not judge them but will love them.

The secret signs of loneliness

- You can't stop binge-watching shows
- Constantly tired
- Unproductiveness
- Feeling misunderstood
- Feeling constantly stressed
- Feeling frequently down
- Fragmented sleep
- Having low self-esteem

About Us

Adopt a Grandparent was founded by Shaleeza Hasham. Having been born and raised on the grounds of her family's care home, Shaleeza started going into work with her mum from the age of 8 weeks – which made for a somewhat unusual, but certainly fun, upbringing. She spent a lot of her time with the residents, keeping them company – and all the while, having the pleasure of 15 adopted grandparents!

Often, our volunteers are those who've lost their own grandparents, and are looking to fill the void and create a meaningful intergenerational relationship. However, the scheme is open to anyone and is a great way to connect with others and reduce feelings of isolation and loneliness.

In October 2019, Shaleeza wanted to take action to abolish loneliness amongst the older and younger communities. The idea initially focused on inviting local people into care homes, encouraging them to 'adopt' a grandparent of their own and make regular visits to spend quality time together.

ADOPT A GRANDPARENT IS A CHARITY THAT SUPPORTS LONELY, ISOLATED OLDER PEOPLE BY CONNECTING THEM WITH ADOPTED 'GRANDCHILDREN'.

Name:	**Chatting With Granma**	Gran'ma Glynis	*(London)*
Service:	*Providing a listening ear, a helping hand and a non-judgemental heart, for those who lack love, because life is a little easier when you have someone to chat with.*		
Contact:	*IG: @ChattingWithGranma*	*E: SignatureHealthPlus@gmail.com*	

You can sign up to become a volunteer with Adopt A Grandparent or donate to their cause.

Adopt A Grandparent
17 Jun · ⊘

Chronic loneliness, when you feel lonely all or most of the time. For the elderly, chronic loneliness can create a serious impact on both their physical and mental health, across the UK 7.34% of elderly suffer from chronic loneliness, we want to get these numbers even smaller. 💙

See how you can help us combat loneliness here at Adopt A Grandparent, head over to our website for more information: www.adoptagrandparent.org.uk/

#LonelinessAwarenessWeek

Adopt A Grandparent
15 Jun · ⊘

Transient loneliness comes in waves of mixed feelings, acting as a feeling that comes and goes. A person may be completely fine one day and then really struggle the next. This type of loneliness in particular is the most common amongst individuals, however, is never really spoken about. 💜

#LonelinessAwarenessWeek

And as for those of you who are godparents now or soon to be, you may be interested to know that there is a resource that you can purchase called 'Raising Up Role Models'. It is likewise a workbook, created with the purpose of reconnecting godparents with their godchildren, regardless of how long it has been since you have last spoken.

The idea is to become the role model to them that they might so desperately seek, as they would greatly appreciate the Time. Love and Discipline you could bring to their life.

Raising Up Role Models is available at www.MartinStevens.me

"The faintest ink is better than the sharpest memory"

P. Reid

Cost vs Value

I came up with the topic for this chapter after thinking about the purpose of this Open Diary being a gift item that you (the grandparent) would fill in with the view to leave it for your grandchild(ren) to receive at some point when they might seem most receptive or able to accept. I don't believe there is a particular age group for this to be so, as all children are different, so their level of care or concern for appreciating this token of love and knowledge will vary from child to child.

The only suggestions I would want you to consider are:

- Would receiving this Open Diary be a distraction for them & their studies?
- Is the content that you will be sharing be age appropriate for them now?
- Can you leave it in the hands of their parents / your children for them?
- ... and do you want them to pay you to receive this Open Diary?

"Whoa, whoa, whoa! Pay me?" You might be asking.

Well, I am a firm believer that people place more value on things that they have had to part with money for, compared to what they receive freely.

The Bible says, 'Freely you receive, freely give' ... but was this book freely received? If it was donated, then fine, but if it was purchased by ... I'm just saying, Ha-ha.

But I am not compelling you to do so, I am merely provoking the thought of (depending on how many grandchildren you have, how many copies you have bought for them, their ages and stages in life, etc) you may want to weigh up the cost value with the sentimental value or even simply use this topic to be a conversation or teaching point about other things with them, whilst simply offering this to them for free.

Things I Can Teach You

Different types of Leadership

There are different types of leaders and ways to lead.

Leading from the front

This is the style of being an example to those following you. Demonstrating the way that things should be done, so that others see what 'good' looks like.

If this is your style of teaching / leading, you are expected to be aware that the world is watching you to see how you handle things.

Leading from the back

This style is very effective because it encourages the follower to become freethinkers, as the leader is at the back watching those in front of him.

Think about how motorbike riders take their lessons. The students have to be in front of the instructor, so that the instructor can see them, guide and instruct them in real time.

Leading along side

Being alongside those whom you are leading, speaks of equality, direct on-the-job training, relationship / friendship and familiarity, which has its pros and cons.

If this is your preferred style of leading, loyalty is important to you, and you must be mindful of who you open up to and how open you become, as you are more vulnerable in this format than the other two styles.

On the next page you will find even more styles of leadership too. See if you can recognise your own leader style among the styles.

LEADERSHIP STYLES

GROWTH TACTICS

COACHING

Coaching leadership is focused around developing subordinates.

VISIONARY

Visionary leaders have a vision of where a company or organization should be.

SERVANT

Servant leaders believe in people first.

AUTOCRATIC

In autocratic leadership, the boss or manger makes all the decisions.

LAISSEZ-FAIRE

Laissez-faire is a hands-off style of leadership.

BUREAUCRATIC

Bureaucratic leadership is a rules-based leadership style.

DEMOCRATIC

Democratic leadership is a form of leadership where decision making is shared with members of a group.

PACESETTER

The leader set very high goals and standards to get things done better and faster.

TRANSFORMATIONAL

Transformational leadership is a style in which the leader inspires and motivates employees to produce a change in the organization.

TRANSACTIONAL

Transactional leadership is a style of leadership in which punishments and incentives are used to motivate employees.

Image sourced from (Common Types of Leadership Styles, n.d.)

How to Pray Effectively

There are a few templates that exist helping others to grasp praying, or rather the prayer structure.   Firstly, there is the well-known 'Lord's Prayer'.

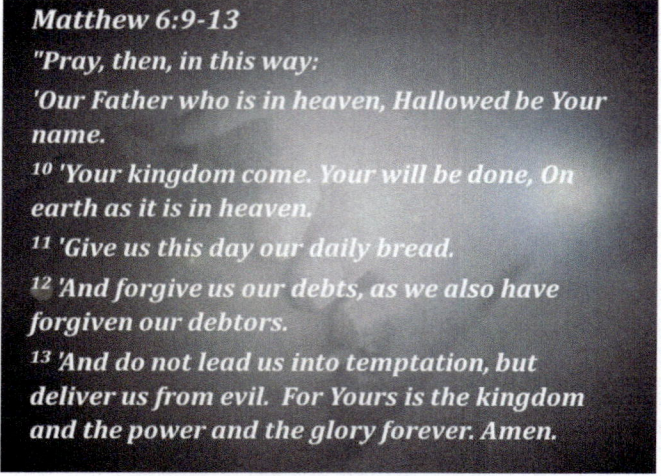

Matthew 6:9-13

"Pray, then, in this way:

'Our Father who is in heaven, Hallowed be Your name.

[10] *'Your kingdom come. Your will be done, On earth as it is in heaven.*

[11] *'Give us this day our daily bread.*

[12] *'And forgive us our debts, as we also have forgiven our debtors.*

[13] *'And do not lead us into temptation, but deliver us from evil. For Yours is the kingdom and the power and the glory forever. Amen.*

Image: SlidePlayer.com (Slide Player, n.d.)

This bible verse has been named 'The Lord's Prayer'. It would be more accurate to call it 'The Lord's Prayer Example, Structure or Template'. This is because the Bible teaches us that we ought not to pray repetitiously. In other words, repeating a prayer over and over lacks effect and validity as the prayer is not personalised.

For instance, if you met up with your friends, parents, employer, whoever, and were to say the same thing to them each time and then walk away, what would the benefit of that be? How would those people feel? What would they think?

Jesus gave us this prayer as a template for praying to our Father, and the evidence is there in verse 9. In fact, read Matt. 6:5 - 15 to get the full context of the story, with particular focus on verse 7, which says ...

'But **when ye pray**, <u>**use not vain repetitions**</u>'

This is because it is a template to help us know what is important to be included in our personal private or public prayer conversation to our heavenly Father.
For an example of our LORD Christ Jesus praying, read St. John chapter 17:1-26.

Here are some more lessons that can be gleaned from the Lord's Prayer Template.

Image sourced from the web:

Space for notes:

Another Prayer Technique

Here is another 'Handy' prayer structure, using your hand as a reminder of the things we can or should pray about. This method highlights topics to remember in our free-flowing prayer. On your hand you have fingers and a thumb, the thumb being the closest to you can serve as a reminder to pray for those closest to us.

- Thumb: To pray for your home, your family, those <u>close</u> to you.
- Index Finger: To pray for those who <u>lead</u>, manage or influence others.
- Middle Finger: To pray for the <u>central</u> government of your country.
- Ring Finger: To pray for <u>married couples</u>, relationships, those seeking.
- Little Finger: To pray for the weak, lonely, infant, <u>vulnerable</u> and poor.

And with your Hand raised, you humbly remember yourself and worship God.

Prayer Types

It's also worth noting that there are different reasons why we pray. We can pray to make requests (petition), asking for something desired for ourselves or others, loke for healing or good health, favour in an interview or meeting, for protection from danger, etc. We can pray to confess something, telling God all about our shortcomings, faults or failures, with the aim of realigning ourselves with God.

There are also prayers of thanksgiving, where we simply desire to show our gratitude and appreciation to God for all that He has done for us generally or specifically. However, the daily practice of prayer speaks to the desire of having and maintaining a relationship with our Father God who loves us unconditionally.

THE BASIC FORMS OF PRAYER

Blessing & Adoration
In prayers of adoration we praise God and acknowledge our dependence on Him.
Example: The Gloria and Act of Faith

Petition
In prayers of petition we ask God for things we need both spiritually and physically.
Example: Our Father

Intercession
In prayers of intercession we make requests to God on behalf of other people.
Example: Watch, O Lord (St. Augustine)

Thanksgiving
In prayers of thanksgiving we thank God for the good things.
Example: Grace Before Meals

Praise
In prayers of praise we express our love for God, the source of all love.
Example: Act of Charity

Image source on Pintrest. (Clare, n.d.)

Family Tree Lineage

Here is a helpful section for tallying the family tree. The name of the grandchild is to be placed in the bottom centre box. You might want to use a retractable pencil.

There is only enough room for first names here, but on the pages that follow this section, you will find blank pages where you can attach names to photos and any other needed or necessary information. There is also space below each tree to use.

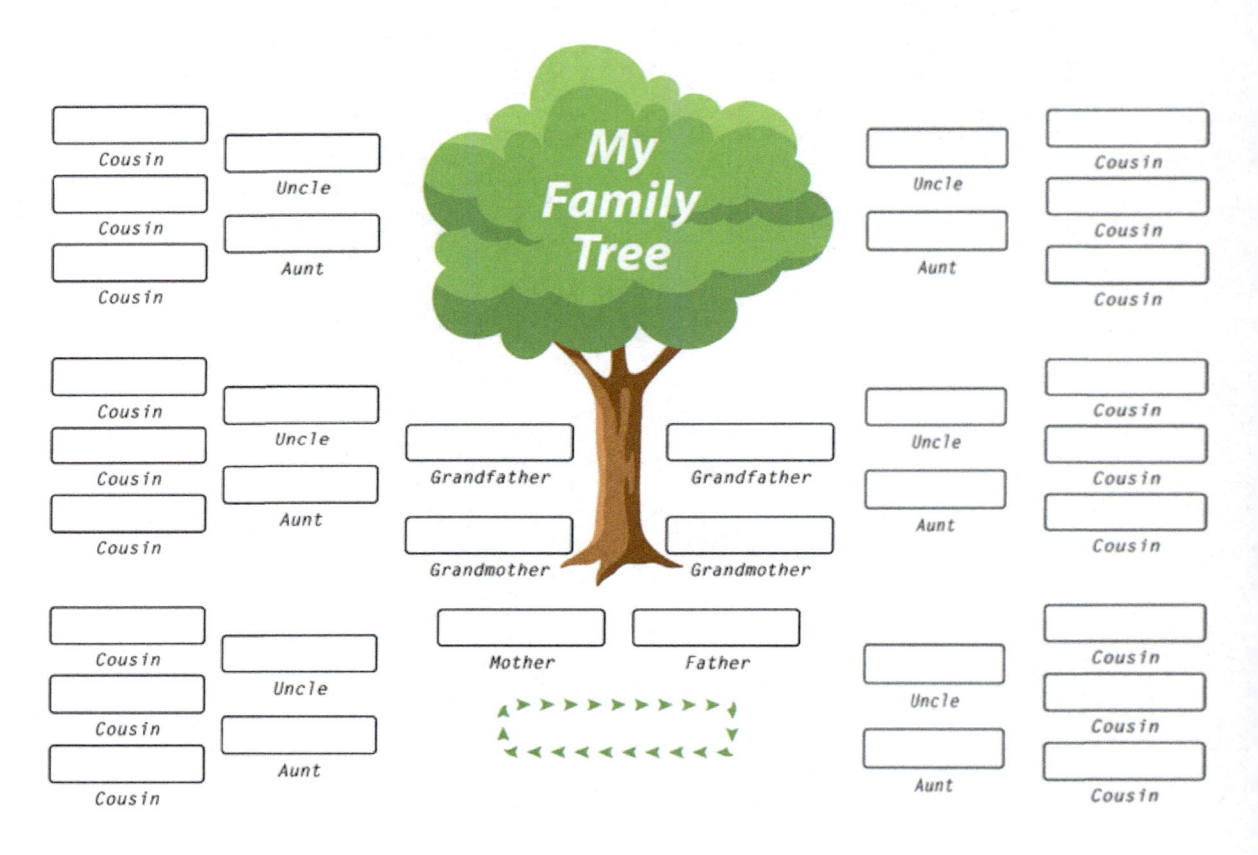

www.FreeFamilyTreeTemplates.com

Space for more relative's names or information. Also, see Directory to search lineage.

Family Tree 2

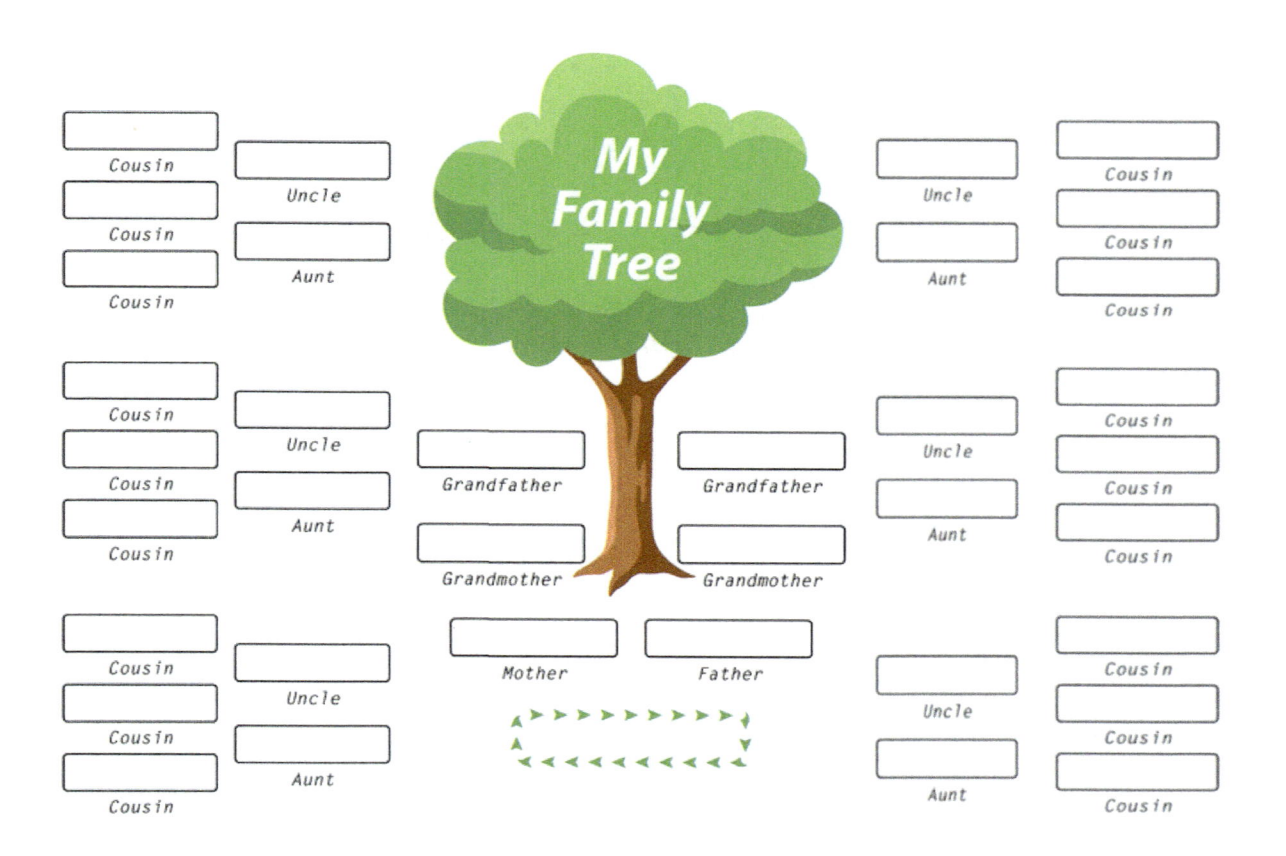

www.FreeFamilyTreeTemplates.com

Family Tree 3

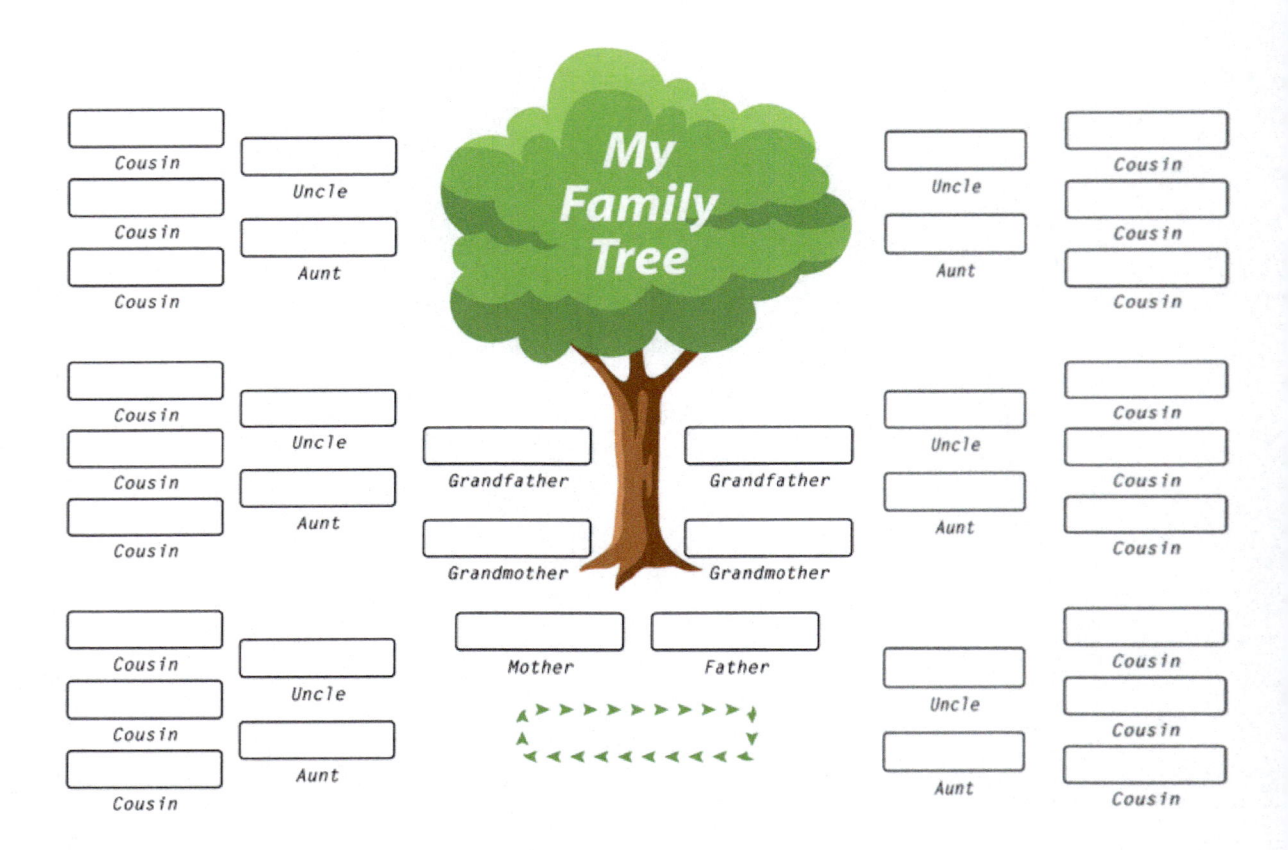

www.FreeFamilyTreeTemplates.com

Family Tree 4

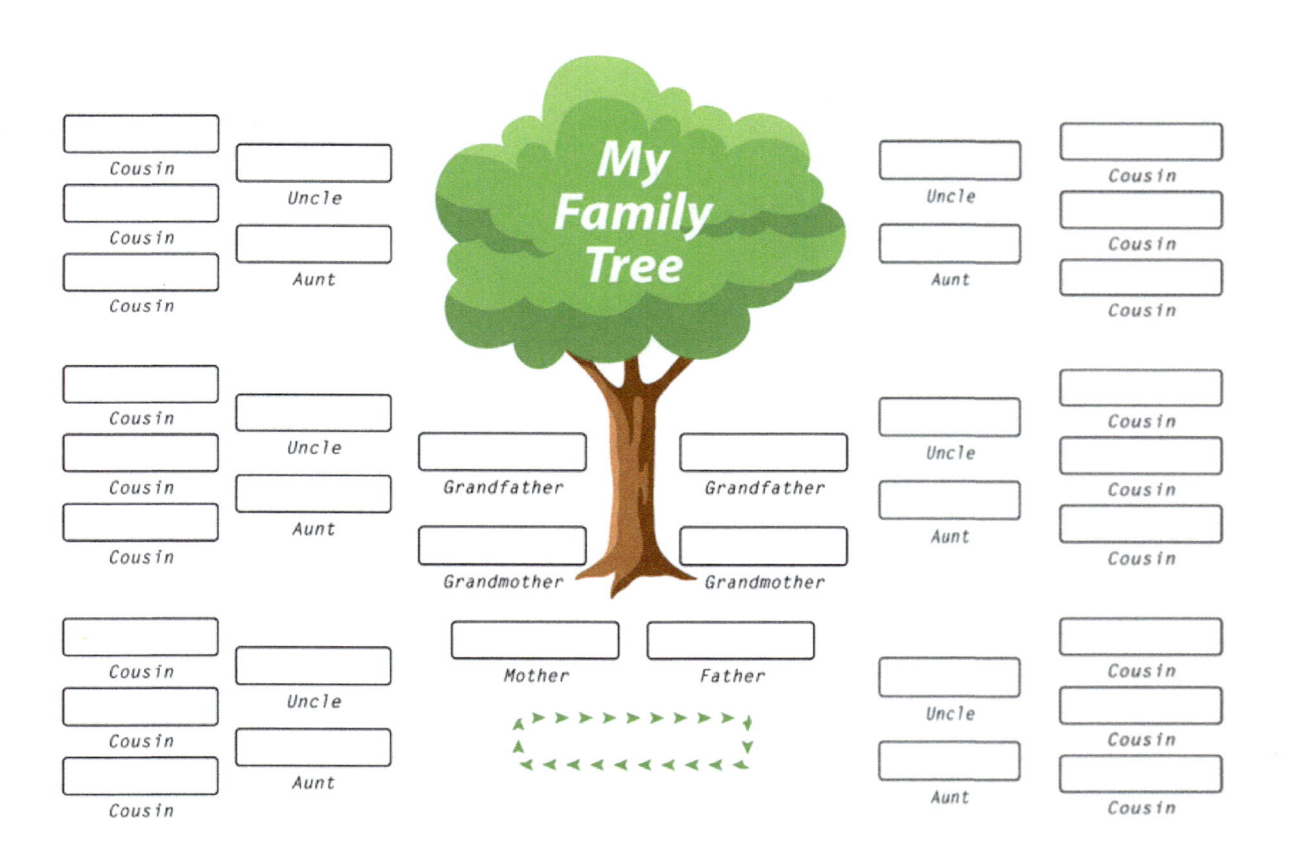

www.FreeFamilyTreeTemplates.com

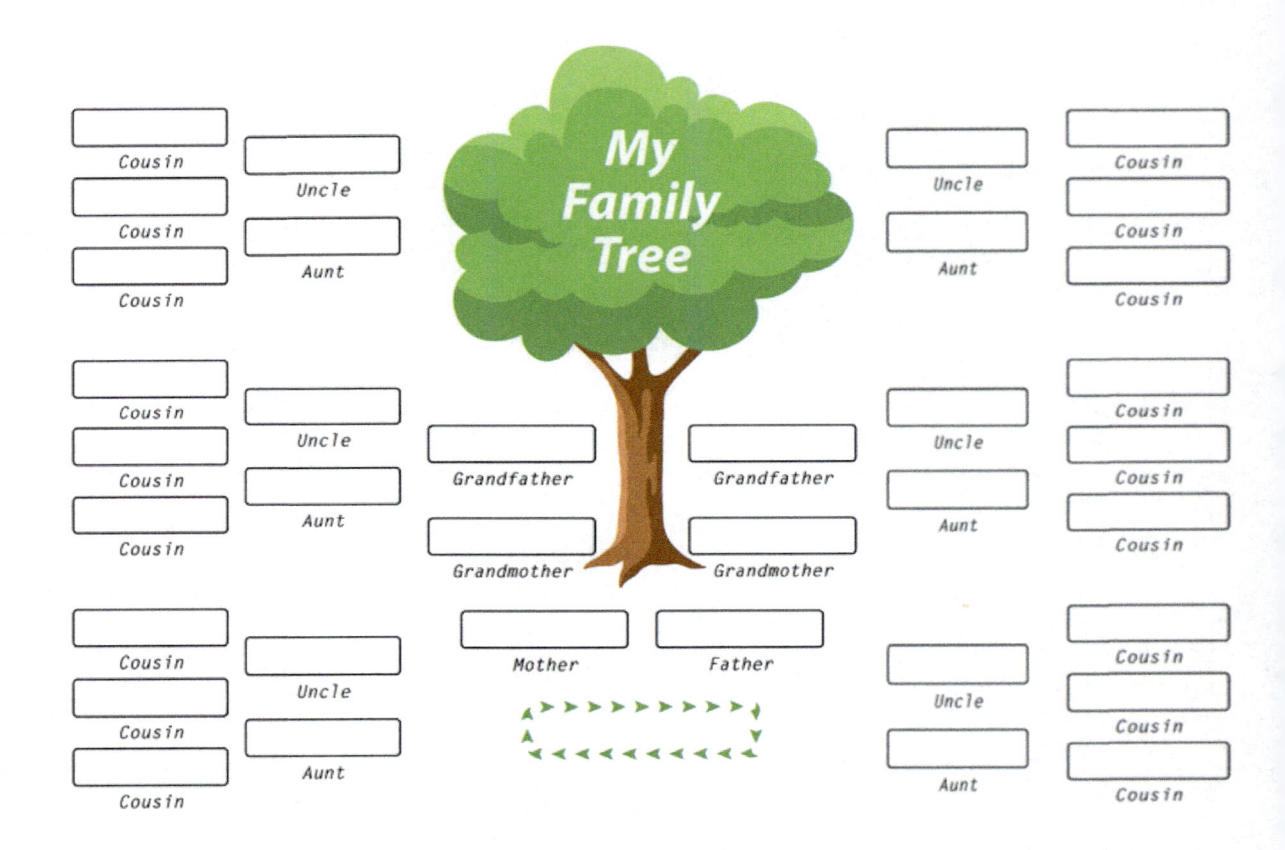

My Family Tree

Cousin

Uncle

Cousin

Aunt

Cousin

Cousin

Uncle

Cousin

Aunt

Cousin

Cousin

Uncle

Cousin

Aunt

Cousin

Grandfather

Grandmother

Mother

Uncle

Cousin

Aunt

Cousin

Cousin

Uncle

Cousin

Aunt

Cousin

Grandfather

Grandmother

Father

Uncle

Cousin

Aunt

Cousin

Cousin

Uncle

Cousin

Aunt

Cousin

www.FreeFamilyTreeTemplates.com

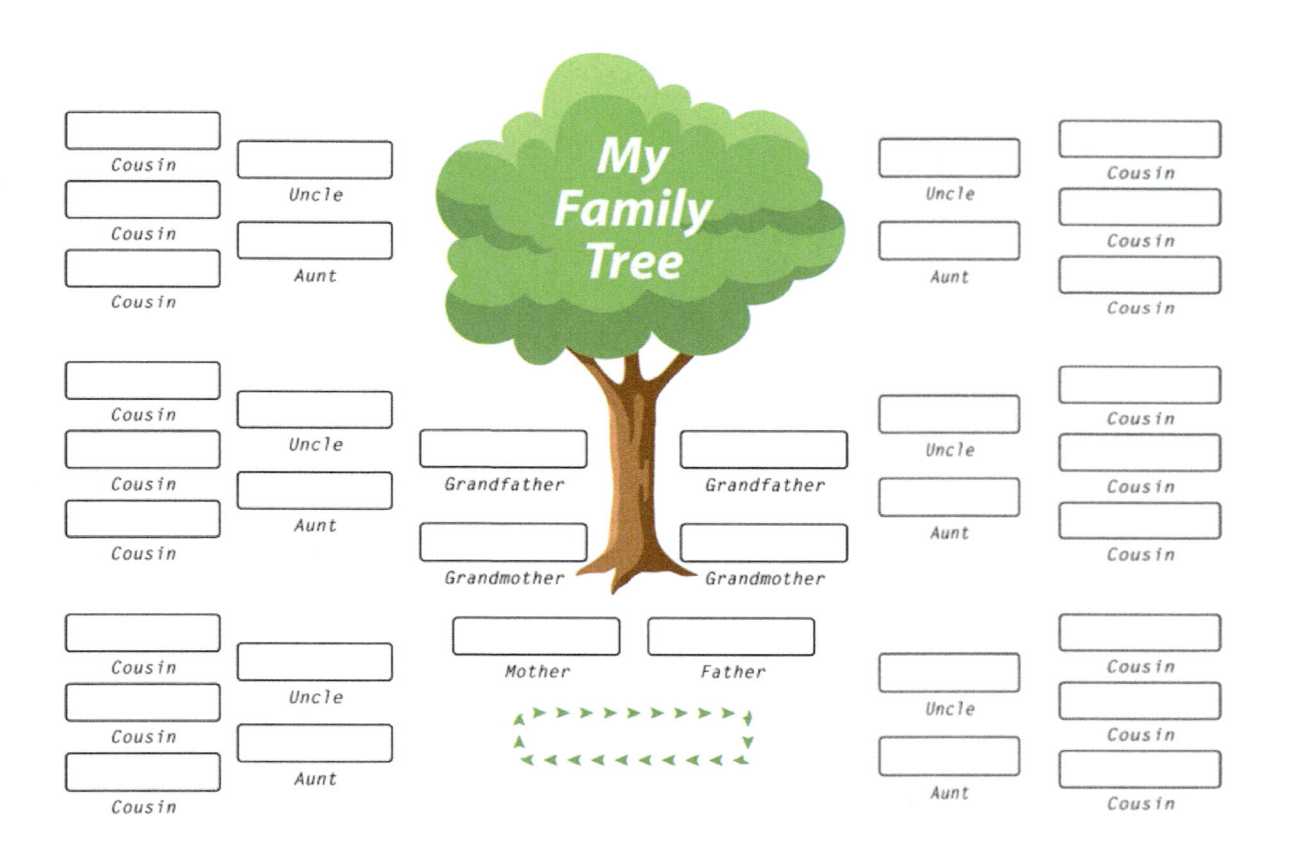

My Family Tree

Cousin
Cousin
Cousin
Uncle
Aunt

Cousin
Cousin
Cousin
Uncle
Aunt

Cousin
Cousin
Cousin
Uncle
Aunt

Grandfather
Grandmother
Grandfather
Grandmother

Mother
Father

Uncle
Aunt
Cousin
Cousin
Cousin

Uncle
Aunt
Cousin
Cousin
Cousin

Uncle
Aunt
Cousin
Cousin
Cousin

www.FreeFamilyTreeTemplates.com

Who's Who

Mum: _____ _____

Mum's mum: _____ _____

Mum's dad: _____ _____

Mum's siblings: _____, _____, _____, _____,

_____, _____, _____, _____, _____.

Mum's aunties: _____, _____, _____, _____,

Mum's uncles: _____, _____, _____, _____,

Mum's godparents: _____ _____

_____ _____

_____ _____

_____ _____

Other special people: _____ _____

_____ _____

Who's Who

Dad: _____   _____

Dad's mum: _____   _____

Dad's dad: _____   _____

Dad's siblings: _____, _____, _____, _____,

_____, _____, _____, _____, _____.

Dad's aunties: _____, _____, _____, _____,

Dad's uncles: _____, _____, _____, _____,

Dad's godparents: _____ _____

_____ _____

_____ _____

_____ _____

Other special people: _____ _____

_____ _____

For any relevant family information, special occasions, anniversaries or stories.

_____

_____

_____

_____

_____

_____

_____

_____

_____

_____

_____

_____

_____

_____

_____

_____

_____

_____

_____

2022 / 2023 Calendar

Calendar & Holidays
2022

January 2022

	Mon	Tue	Wed	Thu	Fri	Sat	Sun
52						1	2
1	3	4	5	6	7	8	9
2	10	11	12	13	14	15	16
3	17	18	19	20	21	22	23
4	24	25	26	27	28	29	30
5	31						

February 2022

	Mon	Tue	Wed	Thu	Fri	Sat	Sun
5		1	2	3	4	5	6
6	7	8	9	10	11	12	13
7	14	15	16	17	18	19	20
8	21	22	23	24	25	26	27
9	28						

March 2022

	Mon	Tue	Wed	Thu	Fri	Sat	Sun
9		1	2	3	4	5	6
10	7	8	9	10	11	12	13
11	14	15	16	17	18	19	20
12	21	22	23	24	25	26	27
13	28	29	30	31			

April 2022

	Mon	Tue	Wed	Thu	Fri	Sat	Sun
13					1	2	3
14	4	5	6	7	8	9	10
15	11	12	13	14	15	16	17
16	18	19	20	21	22	23	24
17	25	26	27	28	29	30	

May 2022

	Mon	Tue	Wed	Thu	Fri	Sat	Sun
17							1
18	2	3	4	5	6	7	8
19	9	10	11	12	13	14	15
20	16	17	18	19	20	21	22
21	23	24	25	26	27	28	29
22	30	31					

June 2022

	Mon	Tue	Wed	Thu	Fri	Sat	Sun
22			1	2	3	4	5
23	6	7	8	9	10	11	12
24	13	14	15	16	17	18	19
25	20	21	22	23	24	25	26
26	27	28	29	30			

July 2022

	Mon	Tue	Wed	Thu	Fri	Sat	Sun
26					1	2	3
27	4	5	6	7	8	9	10
28	11	12	13	14	15	16	17
29	18	19	20	21	22	23	24
30	25	26	27	28	29	30	31

August 2022

	Mon	Tue	Wed	Thu	Fri	Sat	Sun
31	1	2	3	4	5	6	7
32	8	9	10	11	12	13	14
33	15	16	17	18	19	20	21
34	22	23	24	25	26	27	28
35	29	30	31				

September 2022

	Mon	Tue	Wed	Thu	Fri	Sat	Sun
35				1	2	3	4
36	5	6	7	8	9	10	11
37	12	13	14	15	16	17	18
38	19	20	21	22	23	24	25
39	26	27	28	29	30		

October 2022

	Mon	Tue	Wed	Thu	Fri	Sat	Sun
39						1	2
40	3	4	5	6	7	8	9
41	10	11	12	13	14	15	16
42	17	18	19	20	21	22	23
43	24	25	26	27	28	29	30
44	31						

November 2022

	Mon	Tue	Wed	Thu	Fri	Sat	Sun
44		1	2	3	4	5	6
45	7	8	9	10	11	12	13
46	14	15	16	17	18	19	20
47	21	22	23	24	25	26	27
48	28	29	30				

December 2022

	Mon	Tue	Wed	Thu	Fri	Sat	Sun
48				1	2	3	4
49	5	6	7	8	9	10	11
50	12	13	14	15	16	17	18
51	19	20	21	22	23	24	25
52	26	27	28	29	30	31	

1 January	New Year's Day	17 April	Easter	29 August	Summer Bank Holiday
3 January	New Year's Day (substitute)	18 April	Easter Monday	30 October	Daylight Saving (end)
14 February	Valentine	2 May	May Day	31 October	Halloween
27 February	Carnival	26 May	Ascension	30 November	St Andrew's Day
17 March	St Patrick's Day	2 June	Spring Bank Holiday	25 December	Christmas
27 March	Mothering Sunday	3 June	Platinum Jubilee Bank Holiday	26 December	Boxing Day
27 March	Daylight Saving (start)	5 June	Whit Sunday	27 December	Christmas (substitute)
1 April	April Fools' Day	6 June	Whit Monday	31 December	New Year's Eve
15 April	Good Friday	19 June	Father's Day		

Calendar-365.co.uk

Calendar & Holidays
2023

January 2023

	Mon	Tue	Wed	Thu	Fri	Sat	Sun
52							1
1	2	3	4	5	6	7	8
2	9	10	11	12	13	14	15
3	16	17	18	19	20	21	22
4	23	24	25	26	27	28	29
5	30	31					

February 2023

	Mon	Tue	Wed	Thu	Fri	Sat	Sun
5			1	2	3	4	5
6	6	7	8	9	10	11	12
7	13	14	15	16	17	18	19
8	20	21	22	23	24	25	26
9	27	28					

March 2023

	Mon	Tue	Wed	Thu	Fri	Sat	Sun
9			1	2	3	4	5
10	6	7	8	9	10	11	12
11	13	14	15	16	17	18	19
12	20	21	22	23	24	25	26
13	27	28	29	30	31		

April 2023

	Mon	Tue	Wed	Thu	Fri	Sat	Sun
13						1	2
14	3	4	5	6	7	8	9
15	10	11	12	13	14	15	16
16	17	18	19	20	21	22	23
17	24	25	26	27	28	29	30

May 2023

	Mon	Tue	Wed	Thu	Fri	Sat	Sun
18	1	2	3	4	5	6	7
19	8	9	10	11	12	13	14
20	15	16	17	18	19	20	21
21	22	23	24	25	26	27	28
22	29	30	31				

June 2023

	Mon	Tue	Wed	Thu	Fri	Sat	Sun
22				1	2	3	4
23	5	6	7	8	9	10	11
24	12	13	14	15	16	17	18
25	19	20	21	22	23	24	25
26	26	27	28	29	30		

July 2023

	Mon	Tue	Wed	Thu	Fri	Sat	Sun
26						1	2
27	3	4	5	6	7	8	9
28	10	11	12	13	14	15	16
29	17	18	19	20	21	22	23
30	24	25	26	27	28	29	30
31	31						

August 2023

	Mon	Tue	Wed	Thu	Fri	Sat	Sun
31		1	2	3	4	5	6
32	7	8	9	10	11	12	13
33	14	15	16	17	18	19	20
34	21	22	23	24	25	26	27
35	28	29	30	31			

September 2023

	Mon	Tue	Wed	Thu	Fri	Sat	Sun
35					1	2	3
36	4	5	6	7	8	9	10
37	11	12	13	14	15	16	17
38	18	19	20	21	22	23	24
39	25	26	27	28	29	30	

October 2023

	Mon	Tue	Wed	Thu	Fri	Sat	Sun
39							1
40	2	3	4	5	6	7	8
41	9	10	11	12	13	14	15
42	16	17	18	19	20	21	22
43	23	24	25	26	27	28	29
44	30	31					

November 2023

	Mon	Tue	Wed	Thu	Fri	Sat	Sun
44			1	2	3	4	5
45	6	7	8	9	10	11	12
46	13	14	15	16	17	18	19
47	20	21	22	23	24	25	26
48	27	28	29	30			

December 2023

	Mon	Tue	Wed	Thu	Fri	Sat	Sun
48					1	2	3
49	4	5	6	7	8	9	10
50	11	12	13	14	15	16	17
51	18	19	20	21	22	23	24
52	25	26	27	28	29	30	31

1 January	New Year's Day
14 February	Valentine
19 February	Carnival
17 March	St Patrick's Day
19 March	Mothering Sunday
26 March	Daylight Saving (start)
1 April	April Fools' Day
7 April	Good Friday

9 April	Easter
10 April	Easter Monday
1 May	May Day
18 May	Ascension
28 May	Whit Sunday
29 May	Whit Monday
29 May	Spring Bank Holiday
18 June	Father's Day

28 August	Summer Bank Holiday
29 October	Daylight Saving (end)
31 October	Halloween
30 November	St Andrew's Day
25 December	Christmas
26 December	Boxing Day
31 December	New Year's Eve

Space for Photos

Space for Photos

Space for Photos

Space for Photos

My Life's Journey – Continued

Sample questions: How did you remedy headaches / stomach aches in your day?

_____

_____

_____

_____

_____

_____

_____

_____

_____

_____

_____

_____

_____

_____

_____

_____

_____

_____

_____

Sample question:

What do you remember about your grandparents and what they taught you?

_____

_____

_____

_____

_____

_____

_____

_____

_____

_____

_____

_____

_____

_____

_____

_____

_____

_____

What goals and dreams did you have and fulfil? And which are still outstanding?

What was technology like for you versus our phones, microwaves and TV's, etc?

What are your views on courting / dating back then compared to now?

_____

_____

_____

_____

_____

_____

_____

_____

_____

_____

_____

_____

_____

_____

_____

_____

_____

_____

Eulogies

This chapter is here to provide you with a brief insight into the world of eulogies.

What is a Eulogy?

When we attend a funeral, we often hear a brief summary of the person's life, their character, their accomplishments and the impact that they may have had in their family, their community and / or in society. We all will pass on one day, and when that day arrives, someone will stand near to your coffin and read out a brief synopsis of your life. This is called an obituary aka eulogy.

A eulogy is a tribute to the deceased, highlighting the most relevant moments and most significant elements of their life. It is a speech that commemorates, pays homage or praises the life of the person who has died, in order to provide more context for those who knew them to have some final moments learning about the individual who has transitioned.

The eulogy can be read be whoever the family delegate. This means it doesn't have to be read out by family members, as a close friend, former colleague or the church Reverend may be appointed this role. The eulogy may also be divided up to be read out in 2, 3 or 4 segments by different individuals who wish to highlight sections that mean the most to them. For instance, a former colleague would read / talk about their time working together, whist a friend could read / talk about their character, and a family member may wish to read / talk about any life lessons they received from them.

These parts must be agreed beforehand and should each be no longer than 5 minutes, so as to be mindful of the overall run time of the service. (Eulogy Templates, n.d.).

Eulogy Template(s)

General Eulogy Template

OPENING

- Start with a quote about life and death, an inspirational quote or an interesting detail about the deceased, then introduce yourself.
  Describe your relation to the deceased and how you met and knew them.

THE EARLY YEARS

- Describe details of their early life in chronological order.
- When / where they were born, the names of parents and siblings.
- Schools, degrees, training, favourite subjects or sports in school
- Add one or two stories that provide a snapshot of their life growing up.

MARRIAGE AND FAMILY

- Names of spouse(s), when / where they met and got married
- Mention the children, wedding anniversaries and marriage length(s)

CAREER

- Jobs held, names of employers / companies
- Hobbies and / or what they were known for

MEMORIES

- Share something you learned or some advice they gave to you.
- Talk about their character traits.
- Add two or three short stories or good memories about the deceased.

ENDING

- Describe the deceased and how they will be remembered
- Add a closing quote about life lived well and / or death
  In closing, I'd like to share this prayer with you."
  "Thank you for being part of our lives. We will miss you dearly."

When I Transition

'Tomorrow is not promised' so we must do what we can while we can.

Life is for living, to be enjoyed, experienced (within good boundaries) and explored, as there is so much to learn, see, do, learn, hear, feel, learn, read, grasp and learn.

I conducted a survey with a few individuals, just to assist and support my concept, and among the several questions, I also asked what they (as parents / grandparents) would like to eventually teach and pass on to their grandchildren.

Here is the response from Richard Fuller.

What types of things would you like to teach them?   *

- ☑ When and where I was born
- ☑ Where I grew up and played as a child
- ☑ The type of music I liked to listen to
- ☑ The books I liked and read
- ☑ The films and characters I watched
- ☑ The food I cooked and enjoyed
- ☑ The sports I played and watched
- ☑ My favourite comedians and restaurants
- ☑ About the family tree
- ☑ Favourite Bible scriptures
- ☑ How to pray and hear from God
- ☑ Other:
  Love, Importance of education mixed with fun laughter, maintaining their Well-being,

Collectively, here are the results from several participants who shared their priorities of what they would like to leave as a lasting legacy for their grandchildren. Please do note that 'money' was not listed in the options.

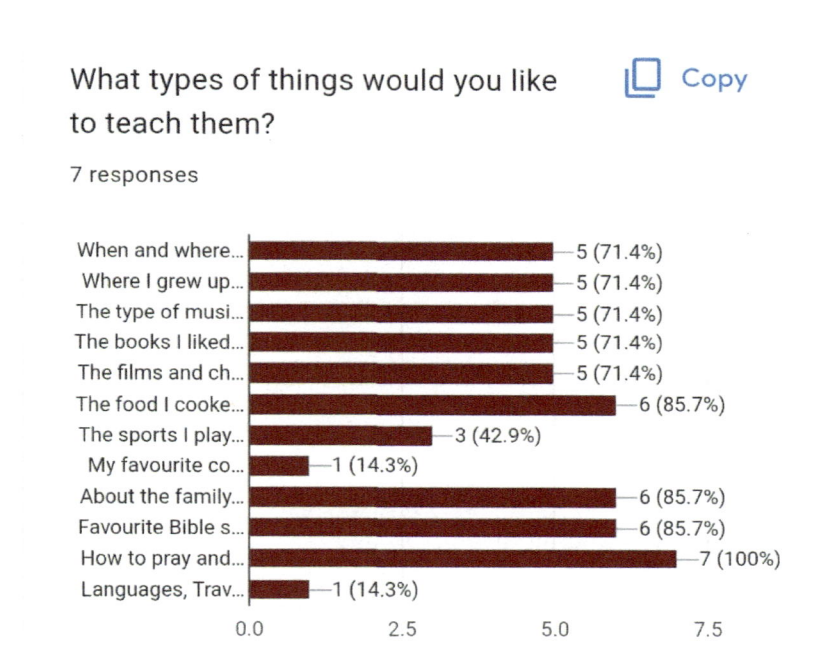

What types of things would you like to teach them?   ⎙ Copy

7 responses

At a quick glance, we can see that one of the least popular options was 'favourite comedians and restaurants' Haha. However, looking at the most popular option among the list that included, *When and where I was born, Where I grew up and played as a child, The type of music I liked to listen to, The films and characters I watched, Favourite Bible scriptures and The food I cooked and enjoyed, was How to pray and hear from God.* This was closely followed by the desire of passing on cooking skills, favourite scripture verses and learning about the family lineage.

We also have some individuals that selected 'Other' and listed options of their own, which included, learning languages, travelling and favourite hobbies. Then there was the opportunity to pose their own ideas of things or items to inherit. Check out the next page to view some of those options.

What things would you like your grandchild(ren) to inherit from you?

7 responses

My religious background, honesty, love, love of books, property and education

Faith in God, my love for cooking and Entrepreneurial mindset!

Wisdom

Good Godly character

How to develop a closer relationship with God.

My faith, cultural heritage, integrity, love of life, appreciation and acceptance of people, strength and resilience

Faith, how to carry yourself & how to treat others, cooking..

Now, this would have been another opportunity for responders to have typed in 'Money', but no one did. This is a great time to remind you that wealth is far different from money.

Knowing that no-one lives forever, a day will come when we shall no longer be around … and when that day comes, the next page will highlight what I want you to know from now.

"Death is not the end. It is merely a stepping-off point" T'Challa: Black Panther '18

When I Transition ...

I'm sure you can picture it. A child loses their parent, for whatever the scenario, that child will feel hurt, rotten, guilty hard done by, traumatised, etc., but this is because they have lost someone very dear to them and maybe they didn't expect them to leave when they did, especially if they were not granted the opportunity to say 'Goodbye' to them.

The offspring, regardless of their age, may find themselves falling into depression, anxiety or all sorts, but to be in a position where you can get to hear the final thoughts and / or the last words. However, there is a way that we can capture these thoughts and feelings for our grandchildren to inherit, embrace and treasure for always, and that is this 'Grand Legacy of Regal Years'.

On the following pages, you will find opportunities to record thoughts and feelings about how you would like to be remembered, honoured and celebrated, but more importantly, to hear words of wisdom, love and comfort, all aimed at grandparents trying to inspire their grandchildren to keep on going, striving, pushing and to expose them to breathe-taking insights, revelations and empowerment well wishes, that can prompt them to continue to move forward, whilst making them proud.

Here's some examples of how the following designated sections can be filled in.
They can say ... I want you to know how much I love you.
I want you to be the best version of yourself.
... to find peace in your heart concerning ....
... to see London from the Shard building.

I want you to know ...

I want you to be …

I want you to go …

I want you to see ...

_____

_____

_____

_____

_____

_____

_____

_____

_____

_____

_____

_____

_____

_____

_____

_____

_____

_____

I want you to read …

_____

_____

_____

_____

_____

_____

_____

_____

_____

_____

_____

_____

_____

_____

_____

_____

_____

_____

_____

I want you to buy …

_____

_____

_____

_____

_____

_____

_____

_____

_____

_____

_____

_____

_____

_____

_____

_____

I want you to do …

_____

_____

_____

_____

_____

_____

_____

_____

_____

_____

_____

_____

_____

_____

_____

_____

_____

_____

I want you to accomplish ...

_____

_____

_____

_____

_____

_____

_____

_____

_____

_____

_____

_____

_____

_____

_____

_____

I want you to travel to …

_____

_____

_____

_____

_____

_____

_____

_____

_____

_____

_____

_____

_____

_____

_____

_____

_____

_____

I want you to find ...

Poem: Separated

"Father, bless me with lyrics as I lay this down.
So that whoever hears it, is lifted up in the spirit,
And maybe they share it with someone who's breaking down.

Wishing that they could laugh. Missing someone who passed.
Father, we wanna ask, why You take them now?!
Leaving us sad and blue. Give us an attitude of gratitude,
That'll do until our faith abounds".

When the sunsets and night has fallen,
I reminisce on all the lives we've lost.
But the process of grief is needed.
It reflects the impact they left.
But there's such a peace found in knowing,
That one day we may meet again,
For with God, there will be no more separation.

"Our Father, which art in Heaven, I'm trying to picture Your dwelling.
They say we've got to forgive other people before we're let in.
As well as living a life that would let us set foot inside,
Otherwise it gives the impression that heaven's just for the nice.

Whilst many struggle with lust of the flesh and lust of the eyes,
How can we enter the kingdom unless we swallow our pride?
I guess we got to be wise, especially in these modern times.
If heading the wrong direction, it's best that we follow Christ.

Remember that we're the bride at the wedding,
Let us abide in His presence, while we're alive and depend on Him to survive,
Until the day that we die and ascend,
We'll look inside for you name in the book of life, and it's then,
Angels will guide us within, they'll reunite us with them,
We'll get excited and spend, much of our time doing anything that we like,
And not sin.

Up there, the brightness is Him. He'll be providing the bling,
Eternal life up in paradise with Your Highness, the King.

By M. Stevens

How to Handle Grief, Guilt and Bereavement

If you have lost a loved one or someone you know has or is currently experiencing this pain, here is a list of 10 things that may offer some comfort to you or those bereaving their loss.

However, it is very important to note that everyone handles grief differently, so this list is only here to aid you with some ideas, tips or perspectives that may assist you or them with managing life and attempting to move forward.

If you do know of someone else going through this tough time, please do season your approach with much grace, wisdom and consideration of your relationship with the bereaved to know what you might be able, allowed or deem appropriate to relay to others from these suggestions.

To hear these points elaborated on, visit Keith Battle's sermon from 25:30 mark. 'Emotion Decluttering, Grief & Guilt' (Battle, 2022), YouTube.

1. God DOES NOT hold grudges against us like man does.
2. God's love, mercy and grace is greater than our sins.
3. Pursue or Get back on your assignment.
4. Love is stronger than guilt and grief.
5. Go to grief counselling.
6. Moving on does not mean you didn't love what you lost.
7. Use fond times as medicine and motivation.
8. Your / Their healing timeline won't be the same as everyone else's.
9. God will comfort you and replace what you lost.
10. Schedule and manage your grieving times.

Bonus Thought: 'Rejoice in the lineage that you came through'.

The lineage of Christ Jesus included the likes of a king, a killer, a prostitute, a shepherd, a polygamist, a trickster, and a prophet, to name a few. We have absolutely no choice in the matter of who we arrive here through, but we can certainly influence our legacy.

A Directory

Here is a compilation of some organisations across the UK offering support for adults and young people. With this list, you can get in contact with individuals or organisations to get help or additional advice for yourself, your children or your grandchild(ren).

There are also spare pages where you can fill in services or organisations that you know of which are not listed in this directory.

A more thorough directory can be found in the directory section of my first workbook '**Raising Up Role Models**', which is available in a few local bookshops, as well as on www.Amazon.co.uk or at www.MartinStevens.me if you desire to buy in bulk at a discount.

They Need You!

Thank you for reading through this Open Diary. Purchasing this book has demonstrated your care and concern for your community, your families and the generations coming up after you.

Our senior folks have a wealth of knowledge, understanding, wisdom and experience that we ought to tap into and document where possible. There are community programs that also encourage this, such as '**Living Library**' which allows young people to meet and sit down with senior citizens and ask them questions about almost anything.

It's the memories, knowledge and wisdom from their lives experience that ought to be captured and noted, if not documented. I remember a quote from one of my mentors, Pat Reid, saying "**The faintest ink is better than the sharpest memory**".

There is also an Instagram page called 'Chatting With Gran'ma, which is run by Grandma Glynis. See her information in this directory under Grandparent services.

List of Financial Service Providers

Name:	**Pentecostal Credit Union** (PCU):	(Nationwide)
Motto:	"Improving the economic lives of its members"	
Service:	The PCU provide savings accounts and loyalty loans for those affiliated with any UK Pentecostal Church.	
Details:	W: www.pcuuk.com	T: 0208 673 2542

Name:	**Aleka Gutzmore**	see next page	(Hackney)
Motto:	'Providing a Financial HUG: Honest, Unique & Genuine advice'		
Service:	Mentoring, training and one to one financial advice. Plus, Mortgage, Protection and Financial Planning.		
Details:	W: www.TheFinancialHug.co.uk		T: 020 3488 1906
Contact:	E: Aleka@MyLifeChoices.co.uk		Insta: **@AlekaGutzmore**

Name:	The Financial Health Coach	(London)
Contact:	Sharon Wint-Gordon	
Service:	Helping families to become debt free and financially independent.	
Details:	W: www.SharonMGordon.co.uk	T: 07956 253 909

Name:	Bounce Life (Ashley Reading)	(London)
Motto:	'Living Today, Protecting Tomorrow'	
Services:	Providing a wide range of Insurances, plus FREE Will writing.	
Details:	W: www.BounceLife.co.uk	T: 07377 463 488

Name:	Eunisure	(London)
Contact:	Andre Parchment: Specialist Protection Advisor	
Services:	Providing home, contents and life insurance.	
Details:	E: andre.parchment@eunisure.co.uk	T: 07944 342 220

Name:	SheDoes	(London)
Run by:	Chrystal Chaplin-Walsh	
Service:	Providing Insurance plans and annual reviews, 121 tailored budgeting advice and mortgage insurance. Also offering exclusive services for young women.	
Details:	W: www.SheDoes.org.uk	E: info@SheDoes.org.uk

Making older children Independent

- ▶ Gradually expand older children's pocket money or introduce it; there is a reason and a purpose. They can learn to budget for their toiletries, clothing, sports and social activities.
- ▶ Work out what you spend on your child in one of these areas in a year, divide by 12 and give this to them as a monthly allowance, add a little bit extra for savings and sweets. Monitor the change in how they spend their own money
- ▶ When they're confident in one area, add another and so on until they're managing all their personal spending.

The Question is... Are you ready to let go?

The Practical
Steps to Mum's Money Management

Collect and Save from a young age

We want you to introduce your child to money and coins as young as possible. Laying the foundations for a healthy money relationship

The Essentials First

Get children involved teach them the value of what they have and embed ways to save money and the environment at the same time.

Confidence & Tools

Provide your child with enough support to be confident. Introduce them to banking and the cash machine from a young age and allow them to budget.

'Go ahead and teach your grandchildren to be good with money'.
Visit **www.slideshare.net/AlekaGutzmore/mums-not-fairy-godmothers**
Slides written by **Aleka Gutzmore: Financial Mentor** (Gutzmore, 2015)

Name:	**Aleka Gutzmore**	*see next page*	*(Hackney)*
Details:	W: www.TheFinancialHug.co.uk		*T: 020 3488 1906*
Contact:	E: Aleka@MyLifeChoices.co.uk		*Insta: @AlekaGutzmore*

List of Debt Solution Services

Name: *Christians Against Poverty*   *(London)*
Service: *A charitable and national company, specialising in debt counselling for people in financial difficulty, facing bankruptcy / insolvency.*
Details: *W: www.CAPUK.org*   *T: 0800 328 0006*

Name: *Step Change*   *(London)*
Services: *A Debt Charity helping individuals begin the journey of bringing their financial crisis under control. Also offering 60 days 'Breathing Space' from debt collectors.*
Details: *W: www.StepChange.org*   *T: 0800 138 1111*

Name: *Get Out Of Debt (GooD)*   *(London)*
Services: *An organisation which explores a number of solutions best suited for you, including the likes of IVA (Individual Voluntary Arrangements) and bankruptcy.*
Details: *W: www.GetOutOfDebt.co.uk*   *T: 0161 523 2857*

List of Fun Activities

Name: **Play Place**   *(Croydon)*
Service: *A fun place to take your godchild(ren) for a great day out. Boasting garden games and exhibitions, multi-sports and soft archery, plus so much more.*
Details: *W: www.PlayPlace.org*   T: 01689 867 366

Name: **Solid Rock Football Academy**   *(Croydon)*
Service: *Providing an coaching and mentoring for youngsters with a passion for football and the potential for greatness.*
Details: *W: www.SolidRockAcademy.co.uk*   T: 07508 053 809

Name: *Beauty and the Brains Events*   *(London)*
Service: *Providing 360 camera photobooths, balloons, cakes and birthday lights, plus many more accessories.*
Details: *IG: @BeautyAndTheBrainsEvents*   T: 07713 235 908

Name:	**Shae's Bunnies**	*(London)*
Led by:	*Shae and Mum (Ashleigh)*	
Service:	*Providing a fantastic mobile petting Zoo experience to brighten and liven up any child friendly event, with Rabbits, Chickens, Reptiles and other beautiful animals.*	
Details:	W: www.Facebook.com/shaebunnies1	
Contact:	E: ShaeBunnies1234@gmail.com	*IG: @ShaeBunnies*

List of Grandparent Services

Name:	**Chatting With Gran'ma** with Gran'ma Glynis (London)
Service:	Providing a listening ear, a helping hand and a non-judgemental heart, for those who lack love, because life is easier with someone to chat with.
Contact:	IG: **@ChattingWithGranma** E: SignatureHealthPlus@gmail.com

Name:	**Adopt A Grandparent** (London)
Service:	Combating loneliness by connecting youngsters with senior citizens.
Contact:	E: AdoptAGrandparent@Picpr.com
Details:	W: www.AdoptAGrandparent.org.uk T: 01386 882 474

List of Pet Services

Name:	**MediVet** (London)
Service:	Offering a range of veterinary services for cats, dogs and birds across their community of practices, delivering exceptional & professional care.
Details:	W: www.MediVet.co.uk IG: **@MediVet_UK** T: 01923 470 000

List of Ancestry Services

Name:	**Ancestry UK** (London)
Motto:	'Bringing Your Backstory To Life'
Service:	Helping people to find, track and trace their family genealogy to know more about where they derive from.
Details:	W: www.Ancestry.co.uk

Name:	**African Ancestry** (London)
Motto:	'Discover Your African Roots. By Black People, For Black People'
Service:	Helping the Black community to know more about their roots, even tracing it back to their royal lineage.
Details:	W: www.AfricanAncestry.com

List of Youth Development Organisations

Name: Heal Hub - www.HealHub.org.uk   (London)
Run by: Lyfe Proof Motto: 'Road To Recovery'
Service: Free online mental health support for Under 25's, helping to
             tackle stress, anxiety and depression across various cultures.
Contact: T: 0121 622 3603   E: MHteam@LyfeProof.co.uk

Name: Set For Life   (South London)
Run by: Sheldon Lawrence-Morgan
Service: Offering mentorship and personal development for young people
             of all ages, plus providing transition into entrepreneurship.
Contact: T: 07566 877 219   E: SheldonL@hotmail.co.uk

Name: Spiela   (Southeast London)
Run by: Ivan Kayima   'Home of diverse collaboration'
Service: Providing online opportunities to under-represented communities.
Contact: W: www.Spiela.co.uk   T: 07904 281 994

Name: Bonnaire Arts Education & Training (Ages 3 - 16)   (Croydon)
Service: B.A.E.T's provides children with high quality, one-to-one performance
             training for their future in the Arts and Entertainment industry.
Contact: W: www.BAET.co.uk   E: Info@baet.co.uk

List of Maths and English Tutors

Name: Private Maths and English Tuition (Ages 6 to 11)   (Croydon)
Service: To help the next generation develop a lifelong love of learning.
Contact: Gailann Houston   T: 07904 108 328

Name: Virtual Maths Tuition   (John)   (Year 5 to 10)   (Croydon)
Service: Daily virtual lessons, with each class having 10 learners.
Contact: T: 07903576 540   E: JohnMatthewsMathematics@gmail.com

Name: Mr Numbervator (Isaac)   (All ages)   (London)
Service: Maths Consultant offering private and public maths tutoring online
             covering Angles, Circles, Trigonometry and Pythagoras for GCSEs.
Contact: T: 07956 819 838   E: Dr_Nosezit@hotmail.com
Details: Weekly Maths sessions held on www.ChalkhillCommunityRadio.com

Name: **Upper Level Tutors**   (London and Global)
Run by: Ms Dennis   see next page   T: 07947 172 069
Service: Helping children to achieve via private tuition for Maths and English.
             Also catering for SEND and offering online sessions. Flyer on next page.
Contact: IG: @UpperLevelTutors   E: UpperLevelTutors@gmail.com

List of Fashion, Accessories and Gifts

Name:	**Golden Eagle and Co.** / **Eagle Empire** (Croydon)
Service:	Providing custom made Teddys, T-Shirts, Flyer designs and natural Juices.
Details:	Insta: **@GoldenEagleandco** E: Annico77@hotmail.com

Name:	ShaCass Designs - by Nellie Bailey Goldson (SW London)
Service:	Providing bespoke accessories and tailoring services for men and women.
Details:	E: Nellieadmira.nd@gmail.com T: 07950 663 856

Name:	Francoise & Co. (Global)
Service:	Providing a wide range of authentic clothing, décor and accessories from the Ivory Coast. Support the Motherland and their indigenous people.
Details:	W: www.FleursDeSaron.Afrikrea.com T: 07512 679 260

Name:	**Juba's Beads** & Amony Accessories (West London)
Service:	Providing custom made wooden-bead necklaces and bracelets, hand-stringed for everyday casual wear to represent African culture.
Details:	Insta: **@JubasBeads_** E: Cadonga@hotmail.co.uk

Name:	**Bagonya** (Brixton)
Run by:	Omaya ABdallah
Services:	Providing custom handmade crochet bags and accessories. Made to order services are also available. Insta: **@Bagonya_Handmade**
Details:	W: www.Bagonya.co.uk T: 07432 425 044

Name:	**House of Hampers London** (London)
Run by:	Jules Insta: **@House_of_Hampers**
Services:	Providing custom-made gift-wrapping solutions of a wide variety of items, including treats, fruits, drinks, candles and much more, all made to order.
Details:	T: 07368 486 239 E: HouseOfHampersLondon@mail.com

List of Nail Technicians

Name:	**Master of Touches** (Brixton)
Service:	A beauty salon providing a variety of pampering services, such as manicures, pedicures, facials, a wide variation of self-care products and spa treatments.
Details:	W: www.MasterOfTouches.com T: 07411 606 862

Name:	**Creative Hvnds** Insta: **@CreatiiveHvnds** (S. London)
Service:	A nail technician providing a variety of nail services, including Gel nails for fingers and toes. Also offering bookings for hair braiding in various styles.
Details:	W: www.my-rev.com/professional/creative-hvnds/

List of Hair and Beauty Provision

Hairdressers   **London**

Name: **Hair By KJ**   Insta: **@Hair_byKJ**   (Upper Norwood Hair Salon)
Run by: Award Winning Hair Stylist and Master Craftsman, Khadine Thomas
Service: Professional hair services and certified educator
Contact: T: 07378 317 165   W: www.Facebook.com/ProHairByKJ
Contact: T: 020 8761 7434   E: ProHairbyKJ@gmail.com

Name: **Anaya Hair and Beauty** + beauty by Mary Kay   (London)
Run by: Award Winning Anaya Kamara
Service: Professional mobile hairdressers and barber services for Afro-Caribbean,
            Caucasian and Asian hair types. Also offering aftercare provision.
Contact: W: www.AnayaHairAndBeauty.co.uk   T: 07949 343 969

Name: **The Merah Group**   (Beauty / Care / Tech)   (London)
Service: Community driven service providers, offering skin care, beauty and
            wellbeing, either virtually or in person.
Contact: Carmen and Semerah   T: 07958 668 204
Details: W: www.TheMerahGroup.com   E: TheMerahGroup@gmail.com

Name: **Natures Natural Hair**   (London)
Service: Providing products for chemically damaged, dry or brittle hair, hair
            growth and more for afro, curly, thick and fine hair types, plus
            consultation services.
Contact: Claudine Collins   T: 07867 434 355
Details: W: www.NaturesNaturalHair.com E: Info@NaturesNaturalHair.com

Barbers   **London**

Name: **Levels Hair & Beauty**   (Streatham)
Service: A barber shop and hairdressers all in one. Providing a professional service
            of haircuts and hairdressing for men and women. App's and walk-ins.
Contact: T: 07956 955 877   **Jason**   T: 020 8677 1164

Name: **Shapes 2 - Barbers**   (Stockwell)
Service: Providing professional haircuts for men in wholesome environment.
Contact: T: 07931 201 474   **Carlos**

List of Herbs and Health Care

Name: **Ital Vital Herbs** - Ledister Green   (Tooting Broadway Market)
Motto: 'Herbs are the Healing of the Nation'   Unit 49-51, SW17 0RJ
Service: Providing naturally sourced roots, herbs and minerals.
Website: W: www.ItalVitalHerbs.co.uk   T: 07894 995 347

Name: **Forever Living UK**   (International)
Service: Providing natural and organic wholistic products that benefit your body.
Contact: Lucy Cann   T: 07881 027 893
Details: W: www.TheAloeveraCo.shop/yPNC6z0k   E: LucyCann22@gmail.com

Name: **Delange Skin and Wound Care Ltd**   (Croydon)
Service: Providing private advisory assessment / advice for all types of wounds,
            skin conditions (dermatitis and intertrigo) and lower limb oedema.
Details: W: www.DSWCare.com   T: 07359 393 789   E: Admin@DSWCare.com

Name: **Pempamsie**   (Brixton, Mitcham, Lewisham and Walthamstow)
Service: Providing African Art, natural and organic remedies, health scans and
            health advice, numerous accessories, books and other inspired gifts.
Details: W: www.Pempamsie.com   T: 0208 671 0800 / 648 4163

List of Confidential Counsellors

- *This is for those who need a caring and
  considerate listening ear or personal prayer
  Please message 07860 121 333 on WhatsApp
  in the first instance to be signposted on.
  Once a contact has been assigned,
  fill in their details below.*

Services Include:
Counselling, Befriending,
Bereavement Coaching,
Mentoring, Domestic Abuse Support
& Pregnancy Counselling.

Name:

Service:

Contact:

Name: The Samaritans   T: 116 123   (London)
Service: 'Whatever you're going through, a Samaritan will face it with you' 24/7
Contact   W: www.Samaritans.org   E: Jo@Samaritans.org

List of Child and Family Support Organisations

Name: Campaign Against Living Miserably (CALM)   (Nationwide)
Service: The leading movement campaigning for suicide awareness, as an average
              of 125 people in the UK take their own lives every week, 75% being males.
              Suicidal triggers incl. debt, addiction, job loss, divorce and homelessness.
Details: W: www.TheCalmZone.net   T: 0800 58 58 58   W: Interactive webchat

Name: Child and Adolescent Mental Health Services (CAMHS) (Nationwide)
Service: Assessing and treating young people (under 25) with anger, emotional,
              behavioural or mental health difficulties. Incl. depression and self-harm.
Details: W: www.YoungMinds.org.uk   T: 0808 802 5544 (9:30am - 4pm Mon - Fri)
Contact: W: Interactive 1-2-1 webchat   T: 0808 808 4994 (4pm – 11pm Mon – Sun)

Name: **Walk With Me UK**   'Connection before Correction'   (London)
Contact:
Service: Guidance for families & professionals using NVR (Non-Violent Resistance)
              approach.   E: info@WalkWithMeUK.co.uk   See next page.
Details: W: www.WalkWithMeUK.co.uk   T: 07883 654 495

Name: ADD-vance   (National)
Contact: E: Herts@add-vance.org
Service: Offering resources and help for family of those with ADHD or Autism.
Details: W: www.Add-vance.org   T: 01727 833 963

Name: **Panda's Tree**   (UK)
Service: A Black / Mixed online community network in support
              network of those with a Down's Syndrome diagnosis.
Details: W: www.Facebook.com/PandasTree   PANDA'S TREE

Name: **Centre of Change Counselling and**   (New Addington)
              Mentoring Service   E: CentreofChangeproject@hotmail.co.uk
Service: Guiding those who need emotional support with a range of issues through
              counselling and mentoring to break unhealthy habits for a better future.
Details: W: www.CentreofChange.org.uk   T: 01689 847 444 / 07758 702 452

Larger List via Online Directories

Providing a large directory of various organisations and individuals UK wide, with a vast
variety of categories and sectors, catering for almost every agenda.

Name: **All The Elements** - An Online Directory   (London wide)
Details: W: www.AllTheElements.co/directory   E: hello@alltheelements.co

Name: **CVA** (Croydon Voluntary Action) **Resource Centre**   (Croydon)
Service: A place for community events that offers office and hall spaces for hire.
Details: E: CVA@cvalive.org.uk   T: 020 8253 7060

Support and Guidance for Families & Professionals using Non-Violent Resistance (NVR) approach
— Connection before Correction —

DO YOU HAVE A CHILD WITH CHALLENGING BEHAVIOUR

ARE YOU A PARENT, CARER OR GUARDIAN WHO WOULD LIKE TO …

◆ Share your concerns with others who understand?

◆ Feel supported and listened to in a friendly environment?

◆ Have information of what to do, where to go and who to call?

WalkwithMeUk has years of experience to equip Parents, Carers, Foster Carers, Guardians etc with strategies and tools to practically manage situations like school exclusions, SEND, grooming, exploitation etc that are due or linked to behavioural challenges amongst children and young people. To strengthen and rebuild relationships within families and communities using the Non-Violent Resistance (NVR) approach

WE OFFER:

◆ INNOVATIVE, INTERACTIVE GROUP SESSIONS AND WORKSHOPS
◆ 1:1 SUPPORT
◆ EMERGENCY ADVICE
◆ ADVOCACY

BENEFITS

◆ Improve communication with child and parent effectively/positively
◆ Increase confidence/self-esteem when challenged with difficult behaviours
◆ Promote selfcare/well being
◆ Feel more supported holistically
◆ Adopt a better understanding within a family setting and working in partnership with the agencies and communities

Referrals: WalkwithMeUk is a registered Community Interest Company (C.I.C) formal programme where professionals can refer parents/carers. Individuals can also self-refer by completing a referral form, which can be found on our website or email info@walkwithmeuk.co.uk

Package: Subject to what service(s) is required, consultation prior to enrollment of an agreed package will be offered to introduce the schedule of the programme and to complete various forms.

For more information/enquiries/costs
📞 07883 654495
✉ info@walkwithmeuk.co.uk
🌐 www.walkwithmeuk.co.uk
Men and Women are welcome!!!

Registered C.I.C   **Lifetime Community Award Winner 2018**

"The NVR Programme lasts a short time but the benefits can last a lifetime"

A wonderful program for Grandparents to be aware of and connected to.

You've done something amazing

Dear Martin,

Donor ID: P2409861X

Thank you so much for becoming a blood donor. You're now part of a very special group and you've already helped us to save and improve lives.

If we were able to take a donation we should be in touch soon to let you know your blood group. Whether you're O- or AB+, the need for blood and its components never stops. Men can give every 12 weeks, and women every 16, so we hope you'll continue to give blood as often as you're able.

Managing your account online at blood.co.uk couldn't be easier. You can use it to find donation sessions and book and amend your appointments, as well as to update your personal info and contact details.

Thank you again, we couldn't do it without you.

David Rose
Director of Donor Experience
NHS Blood and Transplant

Your name: _____ _____ Blood Type: ___ _____

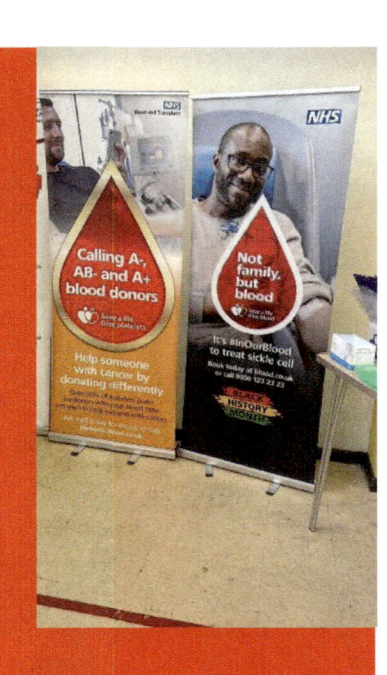

Do something amazing Give blood

Call us on **0300 123 23 23**

Visit us at **www.blood.co.uk**

Like us on Facebook **NHS Blood Donation**

Tweet us at **@GiveBloodNHS**

Follow us on Instagram **@GiveBloodNHS**

The power to help treat sickle cell is #InOurBlood.
Blood donors of Black heritage are urgently needed.

List of Local Community Projects in Croydon

Name:	**My Ends**	(Croydon)
Run by:	Various Croydon Partners, including PJ's Community Services, Finesse Foreva, Croydon BME, Palace For Life foundation and Walk With Me UK.	
Service:	Facilitating community communications, events planning and networking with organisations, entrepreneurs, educators, leaders, ministers & police.	
Details:	Location: CVA Centre, Fridays from 11am – 1:00pm	

Name:	**The Lioness Circle** (TLC aka Lioness Tamar)	(Thornton Heath)
Motto:	'Individually We Survive, Together We Thrive'	T: 07904 875 793
Service:	A women and girls support network for survivors of domestic abuse and sexual violence, particularly those born of African and Caribbean descent.	
Details:	W: www.LionessTamar.com Bookings made via the website.	

Name:	Walking With Giants	(Croydon)
Service:	Supporting youths affected by gang affiliation, crime and disadvantaged backgrounds. Also allowing young people to engage in positive activities.	
Details:	W: www.CroydonCommunityLeaders.com/walking-with-giants	
Contacts:	E: WalkingWithGiants247@gmail.com IG: @WalkingWithGiants247	

Name:	Kooth	(London)
Service:	Free, safe and anonymous online counselling and mental wellbeing support provided for those between the ages of 11 - 25.	
Contacts:	W: www.Kooth.com E: Alee@Kooth.com T: 07878 258 019	

Name:	**P4YE** (Project 4 Youth Empowerment)	(Croydon & S. London)
Service:	Providing events, 1:1 and Group Mentoring, Advocacy and Parental Support. Connecting to 'Engage and Empower' our young people.	
Contacts:	W: www.P4YE.co.uk E: Info@P4YE.co.uk T: 07727 277 431	

Name:	AYW (Aspiring Young Women)	(London)
Run by:	Denise Dickenson	
Details:	W: www.AspiringYoungWomen.org T: 07511 489 852	

Name:	**Croydon Vision Charity**	(Croydon)
Motto:	'Changing How We See' - There is life after sight loss	
Service:	Transforming lives and encouraging people to re-evaluate what's possible when you are blind or partially sighted. T: 020 8688 2486	
Details:	W: www.CroydonVision.org.uk E: Info@CroydonVision.org.uk	

List of Community Organisations

Name:	**CALAT** (Croydon Adult Learning And Training) (Croydon Clocktower)
Motto:	'The home of Adult Education in Croydon' - (T. Heath & New Addington)
Service:	Providing hundreds of part-time courses across 3 venues in Croydon, including creative arts, health and social care, languages and ICT. Learn the skills you need to take the next step in your career.
Details:	T: 020 8726 7777 (option 3 / option 2) D: Monday to Friday, 9am to 4pm

Name:	**Mentivity** (London)
Service:	Providing support for young people, schools and parents through 1:1 mentoring and group conversation-based learning.
Details:	W: www.Mentivity.com E: info@Mentivity.com T: 07484 854 893

Name:	**JFJ Foundation** (Justice for Jermaine) (Croydon & London)
Service:	Educating young people on the dangers of serious violence, such as knife crime through onsite workshops, helping them to make better choices.
Details:	W: www.JFJFoundation.org T: 07859 955 968

Name:	**London First Aid Training** (Clapham South)
Services:	Providing affordable courses on First Aid, plus Mental Health at work.
Contact:	E: admin@LondonFirstAidTraining.com
Details:	W: www.LondonFirstAidTraining.com T: 020 8133 8552

Name:	**Legacy Youth Zone** T: 020 3976 9990 (Croydon)
Service:	A youth zone for those aged between 8 – 19, offering teaching various skills and services, including boxing, cooking and music production.
Details:	W: www.LegacyYouthZone.org E: Enquiries@LegacyYounthZone.org

Name:	**Early Help Family Solutions** (Croydon)
Motto:	"Intervening as soon as possible to tackle problems emerging for children, young people aged 0 - 18 and their families".
Service:	Supporting families dealing with DV (Domestic Violence), MH (Mental Health), substance misuse, school attendance, housing, self-harm, gang affiliation, social isolation and parent/child conflict.
Details:	E: Lorraine.Redmond@Croydon.gov.uk M: 07926 085 410

SPOC (Single Point of Contact): 020 8255 2888

List of Online Christian Dating Services +

Name: Christian Mingle   (International)
Motto: *'Love is patient. Love is kind. Love is here'*
Service: *Helping you to connect with a community of Christian singles online.*
Details: *W: www.ChristianMingle.com*

Name: Christian Café   (International)
Motto: *'Connecting Christians since 1999'*
Service: *Helping Christians singles find long lasting and Christ-centred love.*
             Boasting over 25 thousand marriage results and over 3000 testimonials.
Details: *W: www.ChristianCafe.com*

Name: **AHF UK**   (Croydon, Wellness Centre, 1st floor Whitgift Centre)
Service: *Providing free confidential sexual health checks, plus STD and HIV tests.*
Contact: *Beatrice Nabulya - UK Testing and Volunteer Lead   T: 07836 745 837*
Details: *W: www.AHF.org   T: 020 8663 5651   E: Beatrice.Nabulya@ahf.org*

List of Life Saving Services

Name: **Community School / Safety Patrol**   (Croydon)
Motto: *'Guiding the Route, from School to safety"*   T:
Service: *Providing a street-presence, aimed at deterring crime and minimising*
             anti-social behaviour. Working with the police, to keep our children safe.
Details: *www.CommunitySchoolPatrol.com for more info, to donate or register.*

Name: Mental Health and First Aid   (Croydon)
Motto: *'Making Mental Health Everyone's Business'.*
Service: *Offering Mental Health and First Aid training online and in person, also,*
             allowing participants the opportunity to also become an instructor.
Details: *W: www.MHFAEngland.org   E: MHFA@Croydon.gov.uk*
Contact: Janet Campbell   *Insta: @CampbellCllr*

Name: Chris Donovan Trust   (London)
Motto: *'Changing Lives, Making A Difference'*
Run by: Ray and Vi Donovan MBEs
Service: *Providing transformative education on how to redeem, restore and revive*
             those who do not see the value of life and those whose lives are spiralling.
Details: *W: www.ChrisDonovanTrust.org   E: Info@ChrisDonovanTrust.org*
Contact: *T: 020 8616 5606   M: 07516 752 307*

List of Funeral Services

Name: *African-Caribbean Funeral Directors*   *(London)*
Service: *Providing funeral arrangement services with dignity and care.*
Also offering counselling, repatriation and floral tributes.
Details: *E: Info@African-CaribbeanFuneralServices.com*
Contact: *T: 020 7275 0175*   *D: Mon - Fri 9am - 6pm, Sat half day.*

Name: **Integrity Funeral Care**   *(Paul Mclean)*   *(London)*
Motto: *'We understand, we care, we help you to say farewell your way'*
Service: *Offering order of service planning and printing, floral tributes, musicians and singers, Live 'in-service' web streaming and much more.*
Details: *W: www.IntegrityFuneralCare.co.uk*
Contact: *T: 020 3745 7795*   *E: info@IntegrityFuneralCare.co.uk*

Name: **Rowland Brothers**   *(T: 0800 0789 636)*   *(Croydon & S. London)*
Service: *Providing traditional and bespoke funeral services, arranging transport and venue organisation. Funeral flowers for all professions and faiths.*
Details: *W: www.RowlandBrothers.com   E: Info@RowlandBrothers.com*

In loving memory of loved ones gone on before.

💜 *RIEP: Mtr Dodd, Mtr Daley, Mtr Green, Mtr Meredith, Mtr Pusey, Dcn Wedderburn, Mis. Judith, Sis P. Friers, Sis Hermeinstein, Mtr McKenzie, Pastor Lincoln Wilson and granddaughter Tia Wilson, Pastor Thompson, 'Queen' Mother Magdalene Thompson and The Queen Mother Elizabeth II.*

'Queen' Magdalene (1934 - 2022)

Queen Elizabeth II (1926-2022)

Celebrating their G.L.o.R.Y

Thank you all

I would like to take this opportunity to thank everyone involved with supporting this project, ranging from those whom I was able to interview to those who completed the survey, and now also to those of which have purchased copies of this Open Diary, especially multiple copies.

And to The Creator for entrusting me with manifesting this legendary idea. To God be all the **G.L.O.R.Y**!

Grand **L**egacy **o**f **R**egal **Y**ears!

Other people, organisations or services you know and recommend

Name:

Service:

Contact:

Name:

Service:

Contact:

Name:

Service:

Contact:

Name:

Service:

Contact:

Name:

Service:

Contact:

Name:

Service:

Contact:

Name:

Service:

Contact:

Name:

Service:

Contact:

References

Battle, K. (2022). *Spring Cleaning Pt. 1*. Retrieved from YouTube: https://www.youtube.com/watch?v=U9dN2KiiE4Q&t=1559s

Clare, R. (n.d.). *Roxbury Clare*. Retrieved from Pintrest: https://www.pinterest.co.uk/roxburyclare/types-of-prayer/

Common Types of Leadership Styles. (n.d.). Retrieved from Growth Tactics: https://www.growthtactics.net/10-common-types-of-leadership-styles/

Definition of inheritance. (n.d.). Retrieved from Merriam-Webster: https://www.merriam-webster.com/dictionary/inheritance

Eulogy Templates. (n.d.). Retrieved from Template Lab: https://templatelab.com/eulogy-templates/

Grand. (n.d.). Retrieved from Cambridge Dictionary: https://dictionary.cambridge.org/dictionary/english/grand?q=Grand

Gutzmore, A. (2015, April). *Mus Not Fairy Godmothers*. Retrieved from SlideShare: https://www.slideshare.net/AlekaGutzmore/mums-not-fairy-godmothers?fbclid=IwAR1a-fqpXLutWMKsZvSJq6byAnZVECxaP23i0hzFASfDZQweqtlWAN0nS94

Legacy. (n.d.). Retrieved from Cambridge Dictionary: https://dictionary.cambridge.org/dictionary/english/legacy?q=Legacy

Proverb 13:22. (n.d.). Retrieved from Bible Gateway: https://www.biblegateway.com/passage/?search=Proverbs%2013%3A22&version=NKJV

Regal. (n.d.). Retrieved from Cambridge Dictionary: https://dictionary.cambridge.org/dictionary/english/regal?q=Regal

Slide Player. (n.d.). Retrieved from https://slideplayer.com/slide/11333972/

Years. (n.d.). Retrieved from Cambridge Dictionary: https://dictionary.cambridge.org/dictionary/english/year?q=Years

Printed in Great Britain
by Amazon